Fermented Musings

khcollins

PRAIRIE SOUL PRESS

PRAIRIE SOUL PRESS

Copyright © 2023 by khcollins

All rights reserved. No part of this publication may be reproduced, distributed, or transmitted in any form or by any means, including photocopying, recording, or other electronic or mechanical methods, without the prior written permission of the publisher, except in the case of brief quotations embodied in critical reviews and certain other non-commercial uses permitted by copyright law.

Cover image: Piotr-Makowski on Unsplash
Back cover image: Alice-Pasqual in Unsplash

ISBN-13: 978-1-7779474-7-7

Dedicated to my sweetest love, Evan. There are no words, only endless heartbeats of love and gratitude for you.

Contents

Water (I) 1

Sugar 11

Yeast 25

Spirit 41

Water (II) 63

Acknowledgements 77

xi / xix / mmxx

Have you ever latched onto a thought,
And shackled yourself to it
Thinking it was freedom?

Water

(I)

i / xxv / mmxxi

I am a sponge,
Absorbing all.
And I wonder sometimes:
When will life wring me out?

v / xxvii / mmxxi

A hard man,
With hard problems,
Stares down
At a little girl.

A little girl,
With little protection,
Stares up
At a hard man.

He won't remember
The last words he speaks.
He'll be gone soon,
And won't have to.

But she'll remember.
She will always remember.
And years will be spent
Trying to forget:

Even if you heal,
Little girl,
You'll still make noise.
Still make trouble.
You will cause more problems

*Than you can fix.
You know why?
Because you can't contain chaos.*

x / xxiv / mmxx

Momma was a number,
A number of all sorts.
But she dripped with feeling too.
She leaked like a faucet,
Spilling out everywhere
With no means to turn it off.

She had a lot of love,
But she harboured too much hate.
She kept a tab of wrongs done,
A lexicon of wounds inflicted,
An index of hurts made,
And held them close to her, always.

Even in times of duplicitous joy,
She could never forget.
Though she tried every which way
To rid herself of burdens,
It could not be done.
For she would not let them go.

khcollins

x / xvii / mmxxi

A distinct clinking noise is made from ice in a glass,
And it means a distinct thing to me.
It's medicine that doesn't heal.
An aid that makes things worse.

They say it makes them happy, yet too much makes them cry.
Sometimes it makes them angry. Hostile.
Or, the odd times, wistful and frenzied.
But it always makes them worse.

Sometimes I don't hear that clinking sound for days,
And peace settles within them.
They seem happy. Happier.
And that almost feels worse.

Because eventually the clinking comes back,
And they say it makes them happy.
I can't argue because I know,
They're trying so damn clinking hard.

ii / xxvii / mmxxi

I feel my days are a series of little griefs,
That begin with the end of sleep,
The moment I wake.

xii / xvii / mmxxi

There is a sorrow in me
Which will never subside.
It is an ocean inside my heart.
Sometimes the tide rises,
Flooding the sand I walk on.
Other times it recedes
Into the deep waters of itself.
But it is never gone.
It can never be gone.
It is an ocean inside my heart.

vi / iii / mmxxii

Today.
Today I won't.
Today I won't let.
Today I won't let myself.
Today I won't let myself give.
Today I won't let myself give in.
Today I won't let myself give.
Today I won't let myself.
Today I won't let.
Today I won't.
Today.

Sugar

v / xvii / mmxxii

I cannot tell
If I am wishing for peace,
Craving anarchy,
Or secretly desiring both.

vi / xxv / mmxxii

Relying on you feels like
Living in a thicket of trees.
I am covered,
I am sheltered,
Yet pricked by pine,
And scratched by cone.

I can hardly see
Through the immense
Growth of your leaves.
There are only cracks
In the horizon
Between your dense reach.

And though the ground
Beneath me
Is bursting with life,
The forest floor is uneven
And I keep tripping
Upon your roots.

x / xxix / mmxxi

She's late for a meeting.
An important one.
The *most* important one.

She arrived at the building early,
Thirty minutes to be exact,
Which was fifteen minutes too soon.

She stopped in for only one,
Just one to bide the time,
But one quickly turned into more.

She slams down the fifth,
Empty of all but ice,
And rakes her hands through her hair.

She clears her throat,
Offers her thanks,
And throws money on the wood.

She shuffles out of her chair,
Straightens her tie,
Then mumbles out loud:

Liquid courage,
They call it.

That's what they say.
So why the hell
Am I so fucking scared
All the damn time.

vii / xx / mmxxii

You.
A viper in the grass.
All I see is meadow,
But there you are,
Slithering within it.
I mistake you for a flower,
Blossoming with potential,
But you are only
A bite of reality
Nesting inside
My hopeful delusions.

ii / xix / mmxxi

Wisps of lithe smoke
Rise jadedly into the air
From the end of her cigarette.
Joined in time
By a wilful cloud
Released from her mouth.

Heat from the ash,
Left unflicked,
Warms her stained knuckles.
Smouldering fumes,
Eagerly invited,
Sear her wearied lungs.

Two sets of brown eyes,
Openly concerned,
Stare at the marks on her skin.
Her own set of eyes,
Delightfully glazed,
Remain fixed upon the smoke.

A question is asked,
For the hundredth time,
Pleading an answer that is due.
An answer is given,
For the hundredth time,

Offering nothing new:

You've got it all wrong, love.
I don't like to feel pain.
What I'm doing is
Killing myself with pleasure.

i / xxvi / mmxxi

You.
What is it about your poison
That breeds such dependence
Within me?

What silken escape do you really offer?
Besides momentary pauses,
Anesthetized instants,
Deadened flashes.

You.
What is it about your limbo,
Your abeyance, your suspension,
That I cannot cease craving?

I suppose it is because
My pain does not stop,
Nor shift, nor alter,
And it will never leave.

It isn't an intruder
But a permanent tenant.
And you are a blissful vacation
From my aching home.

vii / iii / mmxxii

Her grandbaby tried to keep it all hidden,
Tried to keep it all from being seen.
But she knew what hurting was
Before the little one
Had ever got a glimpse of it.
She'd already lived
Through a lifetime of pain
Before the little one
Was even born.

So, with shaky fingers
And a sad smile,
She grabbed her grandbaby's chin
And whispered to her gently:

Things were different then.
People were.
We had rougher hands,
But kinder eyes.
Weathered lungs,
But fuller breaths.
Calm minds,
Calm hearts.
But you lot nowadays,
You buzz around more than bees,
And you don't know yet

*How to make honey from the sticky stuff.
You can't seem to figure out
How to make sweetness from the mess.
I hope you do one day, baby,
I hope you do.*

i / xxiii / mmxii

The mask is beginning to itch.
It doesn't fit anymore.
I can feel the edges of my skin showing.
When I shift the cover to hide what's underneath,
Another spot peeks out.

I don't know what this role is any longer,
Or how it's meant to be played.
I'm too lost in it,
Or not lost enough.
I can't rightly tell anymore.

Who are you? I ask.
Who am I? a voice repeats.
I am you.

What are you doing? I ask.
What am I doing? a voice repeats.
I am trying.

viii / xxix / mmxxii

I fall upon these dying leaves
As though they were a bed of feathers.
I do not hear the crunch.
Nor do I feel weightless bliss, though.
I am simply left on my back,
Exposed,
Submissive,
Ignorant, to what I rest upon.

But the cold flat ground
Soon presses against my bones.
The solidity of foundation,
Absent of cushion.
I lie upon my back
In a pile of dead leaves,
And even as awareness dawns,
I do not hear the crunch.

Yeast

iv / xxvii / mmxxii

I am hungry. Starving. Ravenous.
I want to swallow it all, chew it up, spit it out.
I want it to flow through me as if I were vapour,
To take everything and keep nothing.
No, do not fill me up.
I cannot contain it.

But bury yourself within me,
And take it all with you when you go.
Leave nothing inside. Nothing behind.
Make me as empty as I feel.
I will let you. I want to let you.
So will you, please, let me go.

xii / xiii / mmxx

Cravings.
Little itches on the inside.
Tingling and pricking.
Poking and taunting.

It's a playful game at first,
But it soon becomes a menace.
Insistent. Relentless.
Not a game but a chore.

What was once a quiet whisper
Becomes a banshee's hiss,
And what was once passed over
Becomes the altar that you kiss.

v / i / mmxxii

The rattling
Of porcelain
Against porcelain
Rings into the air,
As she carries
Two sets of teacups
Into the living room.
One for her,
One for her guest.
She sets them down
On a table
In between them,
Hearing the
Sharp clutter
Of porcelain
Against glass.
One cup is filled
With coffee,
The other cup
Is not.
She slides the first
Toward her guest,
Cradling the second
Close to her chest.
The aroma of malt
Cannot be masked

By the smell of bean,
But she acts
As if it can.
Later,
When the last sip
Has been sipped,
And warmth
Encompasses
Her body
Once more,
She says:

Sometimes
I feel as though
I am deliberately
Unwell.

viii / iv / mmxxii

One. Two. Three. Four. Five.
Ten.
It feels like heaven
Before fading to nothing.
Sordid.
Dirty.
Repetitively fucked.
There can be no pleasure
Once you're past the point
Of hooked.
Drowning in a wave,
Of permanent disregard,
I just want to stop swimming
But my cravings are a shark.

vi / xiv / mmxxii

He thinks the tears in my eyes,
The sniffles in my nose,
Mean that I've been crying.
I walk into the room
With these symptoms,
And he believes
They are from sadness.
A moment of emotion.
Grief.

He doesn't know
That I've just exhumed
Buried parts from my body.
I have disentombed
Bones that were once inside.
He thinks that I am crying,
And in a way I am,
For I did just come
From a funeral of sorts.

vi / xxvi / mmxxii

Her aching legs shuffle onto
The worn-out barstool,
Scratched and scuffed
From years of overuse.
Sort of like her.
She likes the way the wood creaks
When her full weight comes to rest
On the glossy seat,
Shined down to a fine polish
From the buff of her jeans,
As she turns from one patron
To the next.
She loves the slight rock
The stool makes when she
Places her boots on the footrest,
And one timber stem,
Shorter than the rest,
Tap-tap-taps,
Against the dirty floor.
She slams a calloused hand
Down on the sticky bar,
A signal to the barkeep
To begin the long dance.
After too many doubles,
And a tab too high to pay,
The barkeep looks at her,

As he wipes down a glass,
And asks why she goes on
Doing this dance.

She simply mumbles to herself:

You know,
Life is grand.
I love living it,
I do.
I just have no bloody interest
In doing it sober.

iv / xix / mmxxi

There seems to be persistent
Shredding
Occurring within me.

Not a cut,
Or a rip.
A shred.

I put myself together,
Then tear myself apart.
Shred, rinse, repeat.

The severed pieces
Don't go away, either,
They just gather at my feet.

Little tiny shreds
Of who I was.
Who I couldn't be.

xi / xx / mmxx

How was dinner? he asks me later that night.

There are two stages involved in that question. The first one is enjoyable, and one he knows about, but the second is a painful ordeal, and one I keep to myself.

It's sort of a ritual at this point, though no form of worship takes place.

The twisted rite occurs after the meal.

I slip away quietly, making sure the door is closed after I enter. I never lock it, though, and sometimes I wonder why.

I tie my hair up: messy, careless. I don't care what it looks like, I just need it out of my face. Somehow it always ends up looking pretty.

I take off my clothes, leaving only my underwear. I need it. It serves a purpose. I lift the lid and dip my head close to the water. I try not to stare at my reflection.

I place pressure on my throat: *tap, tap, tap,* like morse code. An SOS that no one will hear. How can they, when I refuse to listen myself?

It happens and I feel lighter.

I tilt my head to avoid getting splashed before dipping my head low again. Bobbing for apples. Bobbing for worth. An oil well, tilting up and down, boring into the earth, trying to bring up something of value. Even if it's only crude and rudimentary.

But it's not working. It's killing me. I hate it. I have no plans to stop.

The clenching ceases and all I'm left with is a mess. But I'm the mess, you see, and what's left is tangible evidence of the turmoil I refuse to heal.

It's not working. It's killing me. I hate it. I have no plans to stop.

Later on, when he asks the question, *how was dinner?* I nod and smile and say:

It was lovely.

viii / xiii / mmxxii

Sometimes I wonder,
If I would still be this messy,
Even if you had not put
All those knots inside me,
All those years ago.

vi / xxvi / mmxxii

I'm wondering.
I'm wondering and wondering
If she can tell that I'm wondering.
I wonder if she can see my frightened curiosity.
If it's stuffed into my grin
Or stretched across my lips.

I'm wondering if she can tell
That I'm dying to ask a question.
Dying to *ask* so that I can *know*.
Hoping and hoping
That a word from her
Will elicit a stop from me.

It doesn't.
Because she just stares back and says:

You can ask me anything, baby.
But it won't do nothing
To answer the real question.
You already know that, though,
Don't you?

i / x / mmxxi

The loftiest columns of confusion
We build our faith upon
Are the things we fear.

But is it really the fear itself
That terrifies us,
Or the *possibility* of it?

What terrorizes more?
The actual presence of fear,
Or the *potential* presence?

We eat ourselves alive
With *what-coulds*
And *what-ifs*.

We feed the parasitic worm
Its daily meal of worry
And it only grows.

It always,
Always,
Grows.

Spirit

viii / i / mmxxii

I thought I was a builder,
But I think I'm just an arsonist.
Burning down my own house
Piece by fucking piece.

viii / x / mmxxi

Nobody understands this cage
I'm in.
Not even myself.

It collapses more
Each day,
Digging so deep
It breaks the skin.

But I only push
Against it harder,
Watching the skin rip,
The blood drip.

Is this cage killing me?
Or am I killing myself
With it?

vii / xxxi / mmxxii

I aggravated this wound.
I know that I did.
I gnawed at the bark
Of my torn skin,
And picked at the scabs
Of my itchy irritations.

No one knows,
For it cannot be seen,
Or maybe it can,
And everyone's gotten
Very good
At looking away.

xi / xii / mmxx

She sits on the peak of a hill and stares out at the sprawling acreages that dot the land. They look like little dollhouses from up here.

All manner of life bustles in and around them, the day's work that must be done. She wonders what is said within their walls, what actions are carried out. Is there love there? Or does hate fume out of the chimney as much as smoke from the fires?

She wonders if they're happy.

Do they punish each other for past deeds? Prior mistakes? Do they know how to forgive? Do they do anything to deserve forgiveness?

Or are they innocent? Pure and good. Does the untarnished heart of a babe rest in the arms of a loving mother?

Are they selfish?

Are they martyrs?

Are they just very, very tired?

Do they feel as inadequate as she does? Unfit for the task of going on? Are they incomplete, like her, or are they whole?

Suddenly, on the peak of that hill, she hears it. The quiet whistle of oblivion, beckoning her to heights of rapture. Serenading her with a song of freedom, of peace.

It doesn't have to be like this, it says, and she agrees. It's what she longs for and in that moment, she trusts the gale's mystical promise.

This could all be over.

What a sad, sweet promise.

One she longs for but cannot keep.

iv / vi / mmxxi

I am rotting.
I can feel it.
You can't see it yet,
Because it's inside.
But you will.
Eventually, you will.
I hope I'm dead
When that day comes,
So I won't see
The deranged carcass
Of my soul
Reflected in your eyes.

iv / xvi / mmxxii

Sunken,
Hollow,
Rasping for breath.
I feel you in the bite of my lungs,
Heavy from infliction.
I see you in the cuts on my flesh,
Deep from fixation.
I have scraped myself
Against broken glass
One too many times.
Inhaled the shards,
Too small to see,
While swallowing my pride.
And still,
And still,
I do not stop,
And hope only for relief.
But still,
But still,
There is none to have,
For I will not allow its belief.

xii / xvii / mmxx

I have changed and he has seen it.

He bore the burden before
With hooded lids,
But now his eyes are wide.

What was so splendidly hidden
Is now dreadfully exposed,
With denial out of reach.

I have changed and he has seen it.

And the worst of it is,
The way he looks at me
Has changed too.

x / xiv / mmxxi

It was a beautiful day.

A cloudless one,
Filled with sun,
A whimsical breeze
Breaking through its heat.

How then,
Did it remain
So impenetrably dark,
In the bedroom of a house?

Burning rays
Poured through windows,
Invading the home
With warmth and light.

Why then,
Could it not
Clear the shadows
Of the person in that house?

Why then,
Could it not
Melt the persistent pain
Beating inside a lonely human heart?

The only clue found,
Rested in a letter,
Discovered
Days later:

You will never understand it, love.
I know that you won't.
You have been deeply wounded in life,
But you remain uncorrupted,
Entirely untainted.
      I.   Do.   Not.

iv / xix / mmxxi

The sterile white walls of the ward
Suffocate.
Deceptive in name,
For they are
A bland grey.
The effects of time
And lack of upkeep.

I note this difference
Only because
The starched whiteness
Of a lab coat
Is held up against it.
The effects of upkeep
And lack of time.

A curious expression
Bores into me,
Demanding something
I cannot give.
Perhaps
That is why
I cannot breathe.

Waiting.
Waiting.

Waiting.
Waiting.
Waiting.
Finally, I say:

Do you know what this is?
I don't.
Can you put a name to it?
I can't.
I just...
I just want it fucking out of me.

iii / xi / mmxxii

She's not quite sure
How to survive the destructive intent
She harbours within herself.

She knows it must be lived with,
All signs point to that being the case,
But she doesn't know how it's to be done.

She asks herself:

Is my life forever to be a battle?
War waged and never ceased,
Onward and onward until…
Until what?
If peace cannot be achieved,
Can I really survive the conflict?

i / xxii / mmxxi

I hoped
That if I wrote it down,
It would leave.

But it stayed,
Remaining in the cracks and corners
Of the broken bits.

The bits I've tried so hard
To mend,
Yet only seem to shatter further.

I am the bull,
You see,
And I am the china shop.

iv / xix / mmxxi

Surely,
Something good can come from all this madness.
Please.

i / xxii / mmxxi

She stood in front of a dozen faces.

Some were strangers,
Without a name,
Some were acquaintances
Of whose darkness she knew well.
More, perhaps, than their closest friends.

She stood in front of those faces.

Hands gripped together in painful protection.
Hands that had made her a living.
Hands that had been her talent.
Hands that had reached for the poison
That soon killed them both.

She stood in front of the faces.

Strangers.
Acquaintances.
Mentors.
Failures.
And spoke of her own darkness to them:

I used to speak.
I used to speak well.

But now I trip over words
As though they were rocks on a path.
My eloquence died long ago,
Along with my peace of mind.

i / xxiii / mmxxi

Everything is falling apart.

The paint has chipped,
The gloss has faded,
From the grip of too many hands.

My threads are as frayed as a tattered carpet,
Firmly indented from the steps
Stamped upon my soul.

I was youthful once,
But not anymore.
I am somewhere in the middle.

Somewhere in the middle,
Of young and old,
Healing and broken.

xii / xviii / mmxxi

Silence.
Too much silence.
A quiet cough breaks it,
Then a squeak from a chair.
A strained groan
From metal dragging
Across a gym floor.
A head nods,
A throat clears,
Finally,
A mouth speaks:

I think the saddest words to be said in a row are:
I don't want to do this anymore.
It's a sad and awful day when you finally accept that
something isn't working.
The level of grief experienced is…gravitational.
It feels like the earth is swallowing you up, dragging
you down into its very core.
But it's not.
You're still there, on the surface. Existing.
And you must continue to exist, even though everything
has changed, the rules have shifted.
You can never unsee what you have finally allowed
yourself to see.
It's not just a realization.

Realizations are easy and fleeting. They can be denied.
But once you accept something...well, denial has no place.
No soil to lay roots in, no vines in which to be entangled.
It feels like winter.
Everything is bare. Cold. Naked. Nothing to shelter. Nothing to hide behind.
It's as open and starkly grave as a frostbitten day.
You don't know how to go on, and yet, somehow, you do.
You can't turn back; you can't stay put.
And so,
Somehow,
Someway,
You lift your achingly frozen foot, and you step forward.
Carrying your burdens that are heavier now than they were yesterday.
You move. You keep moving.
That's all that really matters in the end,
Isn't it?

Water

(II)

xi / vi / mmxxi

Awful as it is at first,
There does come a high from acceptance.

A spark of clarity
You forgot you had,
From years of wading
In the shallow shores
Of aching numbness.
An awakening,
From a blurred existence
Of buffered time,
Buffered feeling.
There's an elation that arises,
Like the high tide
Of freedom.
Known before,
Yet newly discovered.

i / xx / mmxxi

Pushing past pain
Is not the same
As pushing through it.

xi / iv / mmxx

She looked directly into her own eyes
And she saw ocean.
Frothing tides, beckoning forth.
An invitation to enter.
She witnessed ripples of life
Bobbing in and out
Of lapping waves.
She saw stillness.
She saw chaos.
She saw destruction,
And she saw grace.
But mostly,
She saw herself again.

v / x / mmxxii

I have walked along this beach
Many times.
Stung by the salt
In the ocean's grasp
That tickles my toes
At high tide.

The infinite grains of sand
Soothe my scarred feet:
Rough smoothing out rough.
The chafe between my thighs
Reddening with every step:
Smooth roughing out smooth.

It all looks so familiar,
Feels so natural,
Smells so fresh,
And tastes so necessary.
I will always return to this beach.
I must always return to this beach.

Not because it is home,
Not because it is hell,
But because it is me.

i / xvii / mmxvii

I have crawled in the grass of paranoia,
Where a friend could be evil,
And the wings of angels cut and slice,
Not feather, but steel.

I have walked in the jungle of illusion,
Thinking for certain I saw truth.
Feeling strangled by thorny vines,
That were merely flowers in bloom.

I have run for miles down jagged paths,
Never reaching the end.
Finally seeing a new way out,
Only to be turned round again.

I have drowned in the sea of loss,
My lungs choking with grief.
Overpowered by the waves,
Unable to find relief.

I have burned in the flames of anger,
Engulfed by the heat of rage.
Endlessly melting into fits,
The ashes leaving me caged.

So, too, I have lain in the meadow of peace,

My heart beating one with the sun.
Feeling the lightness of my soul,
And the wisdom of being One.

And I have bathed in the river of love,
Basking on the banks of sweet bliss.
Seeing life in its most beautiful form,
Upon rocks of worthiness.

All of these places I have been,
And to all of them I will still go.
For this is what it means to journey,
This is what it means to come home.

i / x / mmxii

The inimical weight of shame
That she always carried
Did not fully lift,
Nor did it disappear.

But it was not so heavy,
Nor so unbearable.
It was not so dense,
Nor so frightening.

It no longer
Impaled her heart,
The grip of its dagger
Cutting too deep.

Though it remained
Within her,
It did not control
All that she did.

It did not silence every word
Needing to be said.
It did not steer every direction
Needing to be turned.

It did not force

Every action,
It did not halt
Every triumph.

For she accepted,
That it never had been,
And never would be,
All that she was.

vii / iv / mmxxii

I cannot return to the place
Before you.
And, despite everything,
I suppose I would not want to,
Even if I could.

viii / x / mmxxii

Have you ever greeted a painful truth,
And cared for it
Knowing it was freedom?

End.

Acknowledgements

This book would not have been possible without the infinite wisdom, profound encouragement, and relentless nurturing of Gram and Gramps. I am forever indebted to you both.

I am extremely grateful to my publisher, Jim Jackson, for betting on me, my vision, and my voice, as well as my editor, Taija Morgan, for gifting me with indispensable knowledge and an easy friendship.

I cannot begin to express my thanks to my mother, heart of my heart, and my father, soul of my soul. The unconditional love, strength, and support you bestow upon me daily are what allows me to walk my creative path with such dauntless steps.

A giant thank you to my siblings, Brianne and Brendan, for always providing both acceptance and challenge, nourishing my confidence and my growth.

I would also like to extend my sincere thanks to the beautiful family I have gained, and the beautiful family I have chosen. You all know who you are, and you love me as deeply and wonderfully as the one I was born into.

And, of course, a resounding thank you to My Mermaids. You are my muses, my soulmates, and my heart simply would not beat without you.

Many thanks to all my friends, new and old, who continue to support my unorthodox self and my quirky endeavours.

Lastly, I cannot help but extend tentative gratitude to the ones who have, and will, hurt me in this life. The invaluable teachings gained from the wounds I bear will forever spark my need to create, to express, and to connect.

Thank you. Thank you. Thank you.

Manufactured by Amazon.ca
Bolton, ON